AF545228

Ultimate Reminders™

FOR COLLEGE STUDENTS

369 Fun, Practical Ways to Make Your College Years Count!

Gina DeLapa

Maestro Consulting Group, LLC
8895 Towne Centre Dr. Suite 105-210
San Diego, CA 92122

UltimateReminders.com

The anecdotes and advice herein are not intended to replace the services of trained mental-health professionals. You are advised to consult with your healthcare professional with regard to matters relating to your mental health, and in particular, regarding matters that may require diagnosis or medical attention. The author and publisher specifically disclaim any liability that is incurred from the use or application of the contents of this book.

Book Design by Monkey C Media

Printed in Brainerd, Minnesota

First edition

ISBN: 978-0-9896291-3-3

To every student who is writing
or will soon be writing a brand new chapter—
may these pages lighten your load and light your way.

Contents

Moms or Dads, if you're reading this book, why not pick up a copy for your son or daughter, and one for yourself? It will help you stay connected and give you a common frame of reference, especially to talk about the issues of greatest concern. You can also turn it into a game—as in, "Pick a number from 1 to 369." Flip to the corresponding reminder, read it out loud, and discuss.

Note to the Reader

This book was previously titled *Stuff You Already Know: And Every College Student Should.* But the version you're holding is so much more fun—and useful.

"Why didn't someone tell me sooner?"

Have you ever wished you could go back to that one moment in high school, maybe even middle school, knowing what you know now? Think of how you would have crushed that test, treated someone differently, or handled that stressful situation with so much more self-confidence.

For better or worse, college doesn't give you the luxury of learning in hindsight—there's far too much at stake. Right when you've been handed more freedom than you have ever had in your life, you're being asked to make decisions with lifelong consequences. But take heart. *Ultimate Reminders for College Students* will help you:

- Discover up front what most students learn only after the fact—so you can succeed now, not to mention five years from now.
- Make the social and academic leap from high school to college, with minimum stress.
- Take the agony and guesswork out of choosing a major—and a career.
- Raise your self-confidence to new heights—starting today.

Along the way, you will also enjoy several laughs, including some at my expense. For example, read how during my first semester at college,

I nearly flunked Highlights of Astronomy (#124). More importantly, discover how you can benefit from my ordeal. *(Subliminal message: I still hate science.)*

From adjusting to dorm life to planning your career, think of this book as a friendly guide to making your college years count.

In fact, if you take these 369 reminders to heart, filter them through the lens of your own worldview, and apply the ones you find most useful, you can shave years off your learning curve, blaze through college with greater confidence and purpose, and graduate to a bright future—*your* future; the one I'm honored to help you create.

Gina DeLapa
America's Ultimate Reminders™ Coach

P.S. Be sure to take the "Are You Ready for College?" quiz on the following page. It will help you get even more from this book.

Are You Ready for College?

Okay. By comparison, the rest of this book is a knee-slapper. But for now, so I can help you set yourself up for success, let's get down to business.

For each of the statements below, circle the most appropriate description. For example, if you strongly agree with a particular statement, circle Strongly Agree.[1]

After you've completed the final statement, I'll help you assess your answers and show you how to increase your college readiness—along with your confidence. Remember, there's no judgment here. In fact, the more candid your responses, the better this exercise will serve you.

Ready?

1. I have a good grasp of what it takes to succeed academically in college.

Strongly Disagree | Disagree | Neutral/Not Sure | Agree | Strongly Agree

2. I make sure my course assignments meet my professors' expectations.

Strongly Disagree | Disagree | Neutral/Not Sure | Agree | Strongly Agree

3. I show up to all my classes alert, prepared, and ready to participate.

Strongly Disagree | Disagree | Neutral/Not Sure | Agree | Strongly Agree

1. If you're in high school, simply respond to these statements (#2 and #3, for example) from your perspective as a high school student.

4. I am able to write essays and other papers at a college level.

Strongly Disagree | Disagree | Neutral/Not Sure | Agree | Strongly Agree

5. I finish assignments on time, without waiting until the last minute.

Strongly Disagree | Disagree | Neutral/Not Sure | Agree | Strongly Agree

6. I know when I do my best schoolwork, and actively set this time aside for that purpose.

Strongly Disagree | Disagree | Neutral/Not Sure | Agree | Strongly Agree

7. I am pleased with my ability to manage my priorities.

Strongly Disagree | Disagree | Neutral/Not Sure | Agree | Strongly Agree

8. I am able to say no, and can do so without apology or regret.

Strongly Disagree | Disagree | Neutral/Not Sure | Agree | Strongly Agree

9. I have identified in writing what I would like to get out of college and I have a written plan to make it happen.

Strongly Disagree | Disagree | Neutral/Not Sure | Agree | Strongly Agree

10. I have a clear sense of my strengths and passions, and how these might translate into my choice of a major.

Strongly Disagree | Disagree | Neutral/Not Sure | Agree | Strongly Agree

11. I have a clear idea of how to explore potential careers, and feel confident in my ability to do so.

Strongly Disagree | Disagree | Neutral/Not Sure | Agree | Strongly Agree

12. I have one or more mentors I can turn to for guidance, especially career guidance.

Strongly Disagree | Disagree | Neutral/Not Sure | Agree | Strongly Agree

13. I have a solid group of people (friends, family, teachers, etc.) whom I can turn to for support when I need it.

Strongly Disagree | Disagree | Neutral/Not Sure | Agree | Strongly Agree

14. I am confident in my ability to make new friends.

Strongly Disagree | Disagree | Neutral/Not Sure | Agree | Strongly Agree

15 I feel tired much of the time.

Strongly Disagree | Disagree | Neutral/Not Sure | Agree | Strongly Agree

16. My stress load sometimes feels overwhelming.

Strongly Disagree | Disagree | Neutral/Not Sure | Agree | Strongly Agree

17. I find it easy to take breaks when I need them, without sacrificing productivity.

Strongly Disagree | Disagree | Neutral/Not Sure | Agree | Strongly Agree

18. My life feels meaningful and filled with purpose.

Strongly Disagree | Disagree | Neutral/Not Sure | Agree | Strongly Agree

If you circled anything other than **Agree** or **Strongly Agree** for Statements 1 through 14 and Statements 17 and 18, you could probably use more guidance and encouragement in making the most of your college experience. Let's take a closer look:

Statements 1 through 4 address academic preparedness. For specific tips you can use to meet your professors' expectations and make your learning meaningful, review the section titled "Rocking the Classroom." Consider getting together with a few friends to discuss these tips in more detail, and to share ideas on how to be more successful. There's power and comfort in numbers—and in group accountability.

Statements 5 through 8 deal with inner drive, discipline, and initiative. Believe it or not, these three qualities will determine your success far more than the prestige of your college or university. How do you increase your inner drive, discipline, and initiative? By setting goals that excite you, making plans for their accomplishment, and going after them with all your heart. In the section "Succeeding Beyond the Classroom," you will pick up several tools and tips you can use to start identifying your strengths, passions, likes, and dislikes.

Statements 9 through 12 pertain to career preparedness. Your professors probably aren't going to take time to show you how to discover your strengths and passions, choose a major you're excited about, and gain real-world exposure to careers that interest you—so I've taken time to cover all of that for you. You'll find a whole section called "Choosing a Major That Excites You," starting on page 89. And, you'll discover how to prepare for internships and a career beyond college in the section "Internships and Careers."

Statements 13 and 14 touch on your social assets. If you don't already have a strong social network in place, the section "Succeeding Beyond the Classroom" will give you several new ideas for how you can change that. And, you'll discover why having one or more mentors can increase your overall success and satisfaction, both during college and in the years that immediately follow.

Statements 15, 16, and 17 help you assess your level of self-care. None of us can survive without it—hence, the entire section "Good Old-Fashioned Self-Care." *With* sufficient self-care, and especially with regular times for renewal, you will feel so much better. Believe it or not, you will also get more done. In fact, if you take breaks when you need them, your productivity will increase, not decrease. Throughout the book, I encourage you to reach out for help when you need it. Far from being a weakness, asking for help can be the ultimate show of strength.

And if you're not getting sufficient sleep, stop everything else and start there. Sufficient sleep is truly is the foundation for success in every other area of life. You will find several sleep tips in the section on self-care. I can also point you to Tony Schwartz's book, *The Way We're Working Isn't Working*, which has a brilliant chapter called "Sleep or Die." For more details, see "Recommended Reads" in the back of this book.

Statement 18 addresses your spiritual core. What better time to start solidifying this core than while you're at college? The decisions you make can set you up for a lifetime of joy and contribution. And that, in a nutshell, is the whole point of this book. Not sure where to start? Check out the section titled "Who Are You?"

PART 1

One Foot In.

Having one foot into college means that even if your boxes are all unpacked, your head might not be. It's okay—getting acclimated takes time. Allowing for this reality will make the adjustment easier. Reminder #1 says it all.

Keeping Perspective

1. Take a deep breath.

I don't want to presume you're nervous. But if you are, it's certainly understandable—you're standing at a crossroads you haven't faced before. Just remember: If other people can make it through, *so can you.*

2. If you live in a dorm, get used to fire alarms.

My first night away at college, before my roommate arrived, I bolted awake to the loudest, most obnoxious alarm of my life. *Welcome to Willard Hall.* Groping for a light, I searched our tiny room, convinced the noise was coming from inside—and somehow it was all my fault.

A few seconds later, as the alarm continued piercing my eardrums, someone pounded on the door. It was John Rompon, my RA, looking terrifically bored as he continued down the hall, pounding every door. *Nice white terry-cloth robe, John-John. Nice tan hairy legs.*

As the whole gaggle of Willardites stood shivering outside the ivy-covered entrance, I realized this was my first dose of college dumbassery. (Dumbassery is tomfoolery at someone else's expense. And no, I'm not British.)

Nor am I saying you should ignore fire alarms—only pointing out that they're not uncommon. That first year in Willard, they were as common as ramen noodles.

3. Take a break when you need one.

Get some fresh air, go for a walk, go talk to friends, anything to give yourself a change of pace and a change of scenery. Then get back to work. You'll get *more* done this way. If necessary, set a timer so your breaks don't take over.

4. If you want to bring your teddy bear to college, you bring it.

5. Check out *Where You Go Is Not Who You'll Be: An Antidote to the College Admissions Mania* by Frank Bruni.

It is filled with stories of people who found extraordinary success outside the Ivy League. (For more details, see "Recommended Reads" in the back of this book.)

6.

Don't pit experience against education.

You need both, not just for a good career, but for a great life.

7. Have a friend with one foot out of college, just as you're putting one foot in. It'll give you comfort and perspective.

I offer this in memory of my friend Steven, a senior at Calvin College while I was a freshman at Northwestern. For two people who rarely had a serious conversation, our friendship ran undeniably deep. Ever have a friend like that?

Two weeks after I had moved into Willard (and had told Steve how much I loved it), he wrote these words in a letter:

"My first couple weeks of college were pretty tough when I was a freshman. I didn't know anyone and I had a weird roommate. But it got a lot better soon thereafter. These are just words of encouragement (but they're true) in case you're a little homesick. If you're not *homesick, please disregard this paragraph and eat shit."*

8. Remind yourself that homesickness is normal and temporary.

Homesickness happens to the best of us. It happened to me when I moved across the country for grad school. (Can you imagine if your second day of classes had fallen on 9/11? *The* 9/11?)

The same things that helped me acclimate can help you: Time. Patience. Prayer. Smiling. Being approachable. Striking up conversations with classmates, professors, and others in the community. Celebrating small victories. Leaning on nearby family (without smothering them) and friends from home. Self-care. Eventually inviting friends over for dinner.

Try coming up with your own unique plan. In the words of Hans Selye, "Action absorbs anxiety." It also alleviates homesickness.

9. When in doubt, reach out.

If something is interfering with your ability to get motivated, get things done, or enjoy activities you once did, it's probably time to reach out to your RA or campus counseling office. Let them help you—that's why they're there.

10. Look beyond the so-called bigger paycheck.

True, there's a strong, positive correlation between levels of education and levels of income. But there's so much more to what your degree can do for you.

College changes your world and the size of your world. It opens doors to new friendships, new ways of thinking, and new ways of seeing yourself. It teaches you how to develop better judgment and make better decisions.

All those tests, papers, and seemingly useless courses end up teaching you how to think critically, solve problems, and manage your time.

Wrangling with housing, financial aid, and the registrar's office teaches you persistence, diplomacy, and self-advocacy.

Finally, college teaches you how to learn, and ideally inspires a lifelong love for learning. How can you be bored when you're learning constantly?

11. Pay attention to how you learn best (e.g., reading, study groups, lectures), and as much as possible, bend your study habits to fit your learning style.

12. For an inspiring look at the true meaning of a liberal education, do a Google search on William Cronon's article, "'Only Connect…' The Goals of a Liberal Education."

13. Don't expect your leaders to be perfect.

Or anyone else, really. Just look for integrity and accountability: the capacity to do the right thing, deal with problems directly, and earn back trust when necessary.

14. Have some sort of written, four-year game plan.

Even if you don't stick to it a hundred percent or fifty percent, you'll accomplish far more *with* a plan than you will without. The best time to make a plan is before you start. The second best time is today.

Anatomy of a Winning Game Plan

The career counselor in me wants to help you set yourself up for success, not just during college, but even more so in all the years that follow. The following checklist is not comprehensive, but it should help you get started.

First Year

- ☐ Meet with academic adviser to review course schedule.
- ☐ Determine if/when you would like to study overseas (hint: don't leave this till senior year, which tends to be employers' prime recruiting season).
- ☐ Tentatively choose overseas program; determine requirements/ deadlines.
- ☐ Visit your campus career center to learn about available services.
- ☐ Meet with a career adviser to establish goals and begin identifying academic/career interests (e.g., through the Myers-Briggs Type Indicator and Strong Interest Inventory).
- ☐ Create a professional, non-template résumé.
- ☐ Learn the basics of writing professional cover letters—and thank-yous.
- ☐ Arrange for meaningful summer employment, internship, or coursework.
- ☐ Start building mentoring relationships with professionals, both on campus and off.

Second Year

- □ Conduct two or more informational interviews in fields of interest.
- □ Consider setting up a job shadow to gain further career exposure.
- □ Declare your academic major (see "Choosing a Major That Excites You").
- □ Prepare résumé for summer job/internship in field of interest.
- □ Attend one or more campus-sponsored career fairs; dress the part!
- □ Continue developing mentoring relationships, especially with professionals in fields of interest.
- □ Start contacting prospective summer-internship sites, preferably before or during winter break.
- □ Conduct practice interview to prepare for "real" interviews.
- □ Line up summer internship; make any necessary arrangements (e.g., transportation/housing, registering for academic credit).

Third Year

- □ Start building professional wardrobe.
- □ Complete career-related internship/part-time job during the academic year.
- □ Revise résumé; continue to develop professional writing skills.
- □ Ask professors, coaches, and employers for permission to list them as references.

- ☐ Identify strategies for making the most of career fairs (see your career center for assistance).
- ☐ Attend one or more career fairs; introduce yourself to employers of interest.
- ☐ Register for on-campus interviews through your college career center.
- ☐ Continue developing networking and interviewing skills.
- ☐ Read books and professional journals in your field.
- ☐ Contribute to mentoring relationships; e.g., through book and article recommendations, professional insights.
- ☐ Start discerning your career plans for after graduation; this may include researching prospective employers and/or graduate programs.

Fourth Year

- ☐ Participate in on-campus dining etiquette seminar.
- ☐ Continue developing your professional identity, online and off.
- ☐ Read daily in your field or profession; consider also attending professional meetings/conferences to further your industry knowledge and competence.
- ☐ Identify what you would like from your work and how you'll find fulfillment outside of work.
- ☐ Continue clarifying your values and interests.

- ☐ Set a target date for having employment and/or graduate school plans.
- ☐ Participate in on-campus interviews through your college career center.
- ☐ Evaluate employment offers/graduate school options; commit to the best one.
- ☐ Celebrate your successes!

Free online bonus: Download the worksheet "Anatomy of a Winning Game Plan" at ultimatereminders.com/free-college-downloads.

15. Ask for what you want, not what you think you'll get.

I was barely out of college when I learned this lesson from a world-renowned negotiator named Paul Tilley. When you think about it, "Ask for what you want, not what you think you'll get" applies to everything from pursuing bigger dreams to seeking out (and finding) the best parking spots.

Paul graciously agreed to be interviewed for this book:

"For college students, negotiation might take place over grades, personal space with roommates, living under their parents' roof after they've lived on their own, and of course, jobs, internships, and graduate school decisions.

And it may take place over long periods of time. Only a very small part of negotiations is about contracts or money.

The first rule of negotiating for me is to make an offer—meaning you need to make sure you put a proposal/solution out there that can be agreed to by the other person; and if they don't agree, at a minimum this will usually get the other side engaged in proposing a solution from their point of view—and now you are getting somewhere.

Watch out for too much discussion over what you can't do—concentrate on what you can and want to do."

– Paul Tilley, Innovative Negotiation
Washington, DC

Free online bonus: Download the rest of Paul's interview at ultimatereminders.com/free-college-downloads.

16. Decide now to learn as much as you can from your life *outside* the classroom.

"As a graduate and a parent, my comments would be to engage in activities that make you more well-rounded as a person.

Participation in extracurricular activities, athletic activities, part-time or summer employment, community/volunteer service, and your church or synagogue are all activities that enhance your life experiences and better prepare you for college and a career after college. These experiences may assist in focusing on a specific major in college and ultimately in determining your post-college career.

The activities I mentioned should assist in developing cooperation and collaboration skills in addition to building your self-esteem and character and that of the people you interact with."

– William R., CPA

17. If you're living off campus, have a plan for how you're going to make friends and get involved.

Often, all it takes to start is joining one good organization—one that's big enough to provide some social opportunities, but not so big that you're never going to meet anyone.

18. Let college be a new start, not simply a continuation of high school.

This holds true whether you're three time zones away, or ten minutes from home. What matters is not the distance but your mindset—and that of the people with whom you associate.

19. To make good decisions, use your heart *and* your head.

20. Ask yourself, "If one of my friends were about to do what I'm about to do, would I cheer them on—or try to talk them out of it?"

21. As much as possible, fight your own battles.

This is how you gain wisdom, confidence, and true self-esteem. You'll learn more from having to problem-solve and stand up for yourself than you will from some of your classes.

22. My mom's advice on how to make your dorm room or apartment seem bigger: Don't overcrowd it. You can always bring in more stuff later.

23. Leave the egg poacher at Bed Bath & Beyond—you won't need it.

But if you cook your own meals, I would definitely get an apron and a good pair of rubber gloves. Don't ask me why, but they make cooking and doing dishes so much more enjoyable.

For bonus points, get yourself some industrial-strength oven mitts—the kind that go all the way up to your elbow, so you don't burn your forearms (like I did, thank you).

Who Are You?

The purpose of this section is to help you think more deeply about who you are and who you're called to be. You'll find the contents loosely follow four themes: conduct, discipline, relationships, and religion/spirituality.[2]

2. While I totally respect your worldview, I have to write from my own—namely, that of a faithful but smart-alecky Catholic Christian. Most of my religious musings are being saved (no pun intended) for a separate book. As with all my writing, filter these words through your own lens, and keep and pass along only what you find helpful.

24. Once you get to college, make sure you psychologically unpack your bags.

If you're running home every weekend or staying immersed in your old life, you're missing out on some of the best parts of this new experience.

25. Learn how to say no without guilt or apology.

Learning to set boundaries and say no when necessary can feel at times like a spiritual battle. But it is also one of the most rewarding lessons life can teach you.

Learning to say no gives you back a part of yourself that should have never been lost. It frees you from the tyranny of burnout and resentment. It allows you to give your energy to the people and activities you treasure the most. The key in *all* your relationships is to find the level that is warm, sustainable, and fun.

Have fun with the tips ("How to Say No Without Guilt") on page 30.

26. Learn to say yes without regret.

Have you ever been on the fence about whether to say yes or no? A few years ago, a childhood friend on the other side of the country invited me to her wedding. Attending would have meant a series of major commitments.

Yet when I listed all the reasons for attending versus not attending, I found that all my reasons for going were noble, and all my reasons for *not* going were selfish. I went. Had a blast. More importantly, my friend and her husband will always remember I was there.

27. You will regret the weddings and funerals you don't attend far more than the ones you do.

28. Once you commit to an invitation, be all in. Don't waffle or hesitate, especially in front of the person who invited you.

How to Say No Without Guilt

Why do we find it so hard to say no? I think it boils down to fear: fear of disapproval, fear of letting go, fear of missing out—on anything. Especially fun. But if you've ever found yourself burned out or just plain exhausted, you know *that's* no fun. So how do you strike a balance?

The hardest part about saying no is not convincing the rest of the world. It's convincing yourself. Use the following tips and reminders to make it easier. Incidentally, you will find more about boundaries in my book *Ultimate Reminders for Everyday Life.*

1. **Count the cost.** If saying yes is going to stretch you too thin, compromise your integrity, or just mess with your good mood, pay attention to that.

2. **Ask yourself how you'll feel about it in the morning.** Ever notice how good decisions are hard to make, but easy to live with? They're also easy to wake up to.

3. **Rise above approval addiction.** That sweet tooth for approval can become a dangerous drug, because no amount is ever enough. What about gaining your own approval?

4. **Own it.** As my old co-worker Tim once said (cheerfully), "I don't want to say grace over a plate of nachos." Figure out what you don't want to do, from watching your best friend's dog to taking someone to the airport, and give yourself permission to stop.

5. **Unless you're in court, don't explain.** Explaining should be optional. If you are going to explain, keep it friendly, unequivocal, and brief. Why give the illusion that something is up for discussion if it really isn't?

6. **Be less available.** Not everything requires a confrontation or conversation. For example, we've all had that one chatty friend or co-worker who needed more than we could give. Rather than embarrassing the person, sometimes it's better just to gently back away.

7. **Be a saint, but not a martyr.** We're called to be kind and fair, but we're not called to take on other people's problems. The people who are right for us don't expect us to.

8. **Let the other person save face.** Once when I was asked to serve on a volunteer committee, I heard myself say (politely), "I need to let that opportunity go to someone else." No explanations, no hard feelings.

9. **Say yes to the best.** This is one of the best ways to say no. When we have a clear idea of what gives us life and energy, saying no in other areas becomes easy, and almost effortless. It might even become a guilty pleasure!

Whether you say yes *or* no, the key is to make your decision consciously, move forward with confidence, and not look back.

29. If you're looking for God, take comfort knowing He is looking for you infinitely more.

30. Rise above stereotypes. Notice how many people sink below.

If you were a goody two-shoes in high school, you don't have to start smoking or drinking or posting nude pictures of yourself. (Please don't.) If you grew up as a pastor's kid, you don't have to carry on like the prodigal son.

31. Be proud of who you are, and maintain your dignity.

32.

Make *your* mark.

You've come too far to settle, or to live out someone else's dreams.

33. If you're pregnant and scared, take heart from those who have been in your shoes and found hope—even after the unthinkable.

Within hours of this book going into production, I heard a young woman speak at church about how it had felt to be a nineteen-year-old college freshman who was too scared to tell her parents she was pregnant.

I share Sarah's story, not to preach but to encourage. Even if you're not pregnant, I venture to say you will find her journey inspiring and hopeful. And if you are (or if you're the father), Sarah's story will be more timely and more meaningful than anything I have written.

Free online bonus: Download Sarah's story at ultimatereminders.com/free-college-downloads.

34. Spend at least as much time developing your spiritual beliefs as you do studying for a class you won't remember four years from now. Preferably much more time.

35. **Let your religious beliefs make your circle of compassion *larger*.**

As a former student of mine once said, “My beliefs affect *how* I serve, not *who* I serve.”

36. Gather a group of friends and watch *God’s Not Dead*, starring Kevin Sorbo as a staunchly atheist professor. It’ll help if you watch it straight through, with few if any distractions.

37. Please don’t judge Christianity by its rock music.

38. **Please don’t use “disciple” as a verb. Or “fellowship.”**

39.

Respect the difference between honest inquiry and mere dissent.

The first seeks understanding, in a spirit of humility, openness, and mutual respect—the second tends to be more about pride, defiance, and winning the argument.

40. Don't argue with people who love to argue.

41. Never fear inviting God into your decision-making.

As someone reminded me just recently, "God wants your happiness even more than you do."

42. Respect the difference between a religion and a cult.

To put it simply, a religion expands your circle; a cult narrows and defines your circle. Religion offers answers; a cult merely puts an end to the questions.

A cult discourages you from thinking, dictates how you should behave, coerces you to shun your non-adhering family or friends, and makes it difficult to leave. Steer clear.

43. Be as well-versed in what you are for as in what you are against.

44. If you're going to excel, you're going to have to leave some folks behind—including, sometimes, the person you've been up until now.

45. Accept that you're still a work in progress, and you still need parental support. Paradoxically, this is part of what it means to be mature.

46. Surround yourself with those who will help you stay on the right track.

"Seek a parental figure at your home away from home. They will keep you grounded and honest at a time when temptations can be at an all-time high. You can find this by working on campus, if possible.

Working on campus has great perks! I worked on campus all four years of my undergraduate education. I was incredibly lucky to call the department for which I worked as a student assistant my 'home away from home.'

I always had a quiet place to study, a flexible work schedule, and a boss who has continued to be my San Diego mother figure. I also had a faculty and staff who always had my back. They kept me grounded and attached to my education/school in more ways than one."

– Lindsay D., recent college graduate

47. If there's something you shouldn't be doing at all (cheating, for example), don't do it even once. If you don't do it once, you'll never have to worry about doing it a second time.

48. Don't confuse guilt and shame. Guilt says, "I made a mistake." Shame says, "I *am* a mistake."

49. Allow yourself to make mistakes, admit mistakes, and ask for help.

50. Let every setback make you better, stronger, or wiser—maybe even all three.

51. Before you flirt with socialism or communism, count the number of buildings on campus donated by a socialist or a communist.

52. Let college make you more refined, not less. My dad says going to college taught him to say, *"That's incredible!"* instead of *"No sh*t!"*

53. If you have to break up, be courageous and kind about it.

Specifically, don't hide behind a text, email, or voicemail. At all times, preserve the other person's dignity. You're dealing with another human soul.

54.

Don't stay with someone out of fear, guilt, pity, or convenience.

55. Resist the urge to share the sordid details of your relationship with uninvolved parties. *You* might forgive your boyfriend or girlfriend—your friends and family probably won't.

56. Respect others' beliefs while upholding your own.

57. Never apologize for having high moral or ethical standards.

58. Respect the difference between imposing your beliefs and exposing your beliefs.

Don't let anyone tell you you're doing the former when you're really only doing the latter.

59. When life goes wrong, go talk to that friend who helps you find the humor.

And after you've vented about what happened, say in your most matter-of-fact, tongue-in-cheek voice, "But I'm not bitter." It'll almost always get you to laugh.

60. Prove the generational stereotype wrong, and trade entitlement for earned respect.

You do this by developing a track record for reliability. *Examples:* You show up on time, well-dressed, and ready to learn/work. You do what you said you would do, when you said you would do it. You meet and exceed expectations. Ideally, you do all of this with a smile.

P.S. It's more than okay to expect the same from your peers, professors, and bosses.

61. Be willing to hear things you don't want to hear, especially when they're in your best interest. That's how you grow and get ahead.

62. See yourself as having (a) more to learn and (b) a great deal to contribute. The first will keep you humble, the second will keep your head held high.

63. You were made for joy and respect. Treat yourself that way.

Where is it written, for example, that getting plastered in college is inevitable? It is, only if you say it is. Otherwise, it isn't. Your choice, your consequences—maybe also the consequences of those around you. Choose wisely.

64. Be confident, but not cocky.

65. You can care more about others than they care about themselves—but I don't recommend it.

66. Don't think of self-discipline as a chore. Think of it as the habit that sets you free.

Free to choose long-term benefits over short-term gains, free to pursue big dreams, free to handle anything life throws at you.

How do you cultivate self-discipline? One great way to start is by making and keeping commitments—to yourself and those around you.

67. If your education is paid for, be thankful but not guilt-ridden. Out of gratitude, commit to one day paying it forward.

68.

Remember that a big part of being **brilliant** is not calling attention to how **brilliant** you are.

69. Keep your swearing to a minimum, especially around your elders.

It's all about showing respect and good judgment—too much swearing too soon shows a lack of both, even when the intentions are good. When I write a book for the older set, I'll tell them the same thing.

70. Don't let anyone besides God care more about your future than you do.

71. Think twice before asserting your age or maturity. As much as possible, just let your words, actions, dress, and demeanor speak for themselves.

72. Accept that everything worthwhile, from getting in shape to getting a degree, involves boredom. Knowing this can help you push past it.

73. Decide unequivocally to be, if not your own best friend, then at least not your own worst enemy.

74. If you truly want to rebel, quietly hold yourself to a higher standard than anyone else holds for you.

75. If you want to be happy, self-confident, and unstoppable, banish the excuses. Life happens to us all.

76. Resist the temptation to make excuses for other people.

As in, "That's just his way!" or "She's nice when she wants to be." Who isn't?

77. Remember that college should be fun—more precisely, fun for you.

If it isn't, something's off. I learned this over winter break, my sophomore year at Northwestern University.

My mom was enrolling in her second semester of grad school at Michigan State, and she asked if I wanted to drive with her to East Lansing. Back then, you had to register for classes in person.

For me, the trip was a chance to spend car time with my mom and to see a couple of lifelong friends. I soon found out Michigan State University was more than a beautiful campus, it was a brand. It was my future.

I know you're supposed to choose a school based on its academic excellence and commitment to world transformation, and Michigan State had both.

But as I sat visiting with my friend Mike over breakfast in the student union, what really lit me up was discovering those sugar packets with the big green Spartan "S."

Don't ask me why it struck such a chord—but suddenly Michigan State, my parents' alma mater, was starting to feel like home.

Six months later, I received my acceptance letter, and two years after that, my diploma.

Moral of the story: Go where you'll be happy *and* successful; challenged, but not undermined.

78. Don't look for the exotic answers, especially when making decisions that are life-altering. Look for the answers closest to your heart.

79. Think three times before getting a tattoo.

To use an old expression, "A tattoo is a permanent reminder of a temporary feeling." Or as my friend Jody said, "It's such a commitment, you know?"

80.

Transfer to another school as a last resort, not a first.

But once you've made your decision,
don't second-guess it.

PART 2
Both Feet In.

Having both feet in means you've gotten past the initial adjustments—ironically, this is when college can start to get tougher.

You might find it helpful to jump ahead to #345 on Oberg's Stages of Assimilation. Though written for people transitioning to another country, these stages can help you make sense of *any* adjustment, including the one you're going through right now.

Rocking the Classroom

If it hasn't sunken in yet, it soon will: College is harder than high school. Not only are the classes harder, no one's there to make sure you study, or even go to class.

But with the right habits, you can more than rise to the occasion. You can show yourself you have what it takes to succeed in an arena far bigger than the one you left behind. This might be the most rewarding, enduring lesson of your college career.

81. Remind yourself as often as necessary, *"College isn't 13th grade."* If necessary, set a daily reminder on your phone.

82. Read Adam Robinson's book, *What Smart Students Know.*[3]

You'll discover better ways to read, take notes, and truly learn (not just regurgitate). You'll go from merely studying for tests to rehearsing for tests—and if your experience is anything like mine, you'll be amazed at the difference this makes in your confidence and grades.

83. Find a study-skills seminar, workshop, or class.

Somebody on your campus offers one. Your job is to track it down and see if it behooves you to sign up. Which brings us to our next point ...

3. For more suggestions, check out the "Recommended Reads" list in the back of this book.

84. When in doubt, Google something. We have more information available to us than ever before. Why not use it?

85. Resist the temptation to skip class just because you can.

This is especially hard in the beginning, when you're new to college and still getting used to all that freedom. No one else is telling you to go to bed, get up, show up, or show up ready to learn. So if you want these things to happen, it looks as though it's on you to make them happen.

"Attend your classes. Do not count on anyone else to give you the information. If something key is forgotten, it is completely on you. Take notes. Again, invaluable. Using a recording device is a great idea, only if you actually listen to it."

– Ellie Ramos, grad-school classmate and hiring manager for over twenty-five years

86. Don't ask your professors and advisers for information you could have easily found online.

Your resourcefulness will be noticed and appreciated. Why? It shows you're smart and respectful (a rare and beautiful combination).

87. For each of your classes, form a team with a few like-minded classmates.

Lean on each other when you have questions. Compare notes (literally), because everyone hears information differently. Get together and quiz each other on material that's likely to be on exams.

I did that last part for my first grad-school midterm. Scored a 96%. Way better than my first undergrad midterm (see #124).

10 Things *Not* to Say to Your Professor

1. "Are we doing anything important today in class?"
2. "What did I miss?" (or my favorite, "Can you send me what I missed?")
3. "Is this going to be on the test?"
4. "My mom thinks I deserve a better grade."
5. "Today's my birthday—do I have to come to class?"
6. "How was I supposed to know?" (about anything that was on your syllabus)
7. "Are you going to give us the notes?"
8. "Can I have an extension?" (especially on or after the deadline)
9. "Can I borrow a pen?"
10. "Hey."

Think of it this way: Every professor has dozens, even hundreds of students. So they've heard these lines and ones like them, ad nauseam.

Bottom line: If you want to be remembered favorably, go out of your way to be respectful, resourceful, and cheerfully low-maintenance.

88. Ask one of your classmates what you missed, and if necessary, ask your professor or TA to clarify the fine details.

89. Sit in front, which helps put most of the distractions behind you and all but forces you to stay focused.

90. Let your hair, clothing, and body language show you care.

You'll stand out to your professors and advisers, even if they dress in faded jeans and baseball caps. More importantly, you'll feel better about yourself.

91. Get a separate three-ring binder for each class, preferably the kind with a clear plastic sleeve cover, so you can keep your syllabus/key deadlines in full view. (Corny, but effective.)

92. Make friends with your syllabi. You can even name them if you'd like.

"This document is the key to assisting you in being successful in any course. Upon receipt, immediately analyze and place all the requirements in your calendar. Do not miss these timelines. Anything you can get done sooner, do it. It's that much less you'll need to worry about later."

– Ellie Ramos, grad-school classmate

93. Get the best grades you can, without compromising your integrity or long-term sanity.

I used to keep a postcard taped to my office wall: It showed a cartoon of a guy waking up to the reality, "Nobody cares about your GPA."

That's almost true. Admissions officers care. Some employers care (some, probably more than they should).

Here's who else cares: *you*. For better or worse, you will remember your GPA, long after you graduate. That alone is reason to give it your best.

94. Go see your professors during office hours.

Building a personal connection, particularly if you present yourself well, can only help. Among other things, it will probably increase your interest in your classes, which will make them easier and more enjoyable.

95. As the saying goes, "Dig your well before you're thirsty."

Visiting your professors might not win you any special favors, but you're more likely to get a break when you need it if your professors know you to be a caring, conscientious student.

96.

Take the best public speaking course you can find, on campus or off.

Most people are either afraid of public speaking, not very good at it, or both. So if you overcome your fears and learn how to speak well, you will greatly increase your self-confidence—and your opportunities.

97. Stay in touch with your professors after you graduate—especially those in your major.

Good professors can serve as valued mentors. There's something deeply comforting about sharing your life and career path with those who first knew you as a student.

It's also easier to ask for (and receive) letters of recommendation when you've taken time to maintain the relationships before you need something.

98. Don't end a presentation with the Q&A.

You lose control of your final impression and test the patience of your audience. I have seen otherwise good presentations fizzle out because the presenter took an endless stream of questions of diminishing value to the group.

Better to say, "Before we wrap up, let's open up the floor for a few questions." Then close with a meaningful story, quotation, or call to action.

99. Figure out, with the help of a professional, which colors look best on you.

If money is tight, you can do a Google search on "color analysis" and probably find some free tools online. You can also visit a department store and ask an experienced salesperson to assist you.

100. When in doubt about what color to wear, choose navy. More than once when I've worn a black suit, I've gotten the question, "Who died?"

101. Be strategic about your mix of classes. Don't overload yourself in any one area if you don't have to.

102. Be friendly toward your instructors, but don't try to be friends—and definitely not more than friends.

For one thing, these folks are grading your work. Which means there's a power differential. As my college roommate Ginna would say, "Honey, no."

103. Be leery if an instructor tries to get too friendly with you—even if the attraction is mutual. *You* have to have boundaries, even if Professor Goodbody does not.

104. Don't confuse kissing up with showing respect.

It isn't kissing up to do the best work you can, smile, show up on time, say thank you, and otherwise treat professors like human beings.

105. Give guest speakers a break, especially on written evaluations. Few of us enjoy rubbing tire tracks out of our back.

106. Make sure you're using DropBox, Time Machine, or some other tool to preserve your computer files. As I once learned the hard way, "Jesus saves, but Moses backs up."

107. Don't do anything that undermines your classmates' ability to learn or your professor's ability to teach.

Examples include texting, typing, talking out of turn, whispering, and web-surfing.

Special thanks to my mentor, Dr. J, for teaching me this principle.

108. If you major in international relations, get some meaningful international experience while you're still in school—even if it's not required.

109.

Listen to your academic adviser, but **trust** no one more than **yourself.**

10 Smart Ways to Make a Good Impression in the Classroom

1. Keep your eating to a minimum. At the very least, don't bring an apple. Likewise for carrots, crunchy tacos, and anything stinky.
2. Dress respectfully. No cleavage, see-through tops, or crude t-shirts.
3. Show up early and prepared. Give yourself time to settle in.
4. Silence your phone and leave it out of sight.
5. Stay awake and alert.
6. Participate, but don't dominate.
7. Be back on time (early) for breaks.
8. If you come in late, slip in quietly.
9. Give your attention to the person who is speaking.
10. Don't start packing till class is dismissed.

Following these tips helped me walk away from psychopharmacology class with a B+, when I otherwise might not have earned more than a B–.

110. Set a target date for graduation, and do your best to stick to it. Be intentional. It's part of the story you'll take with you.

111. We all get bored in class sometimes. The key is not to show it.

Smiling helps. So does sitting up straight. By acting interested, you might find you *become* interested.

112. For a good look at how to use PowerPoint sparingly and effectively, read *Presentation Zen* by Garr Reynolds.

113. Try not to take Intro to Marketing at 8:00 a.m. in the dead of winter. Why make life harder than it is?

114. Take a tough, practical writing course.

If you can write well, you can be heard. If you can be heard, you can have an influence. If you can have an influence, you can change the world in ways you care about.

115. Steer clear of professors who use their role to promote a personal agenda, bash your parents, or bash anyone/anything else you hold dear.

116. If you're going to ask for a better grade, make sure your reasons are merit-based, not simply related to stress, circumstance, or how hard you worked.

117. Don't fault a professor for being demanding in a good way. A good professor, like a good coach or parent, will challenge you, support you, and leave you better than you were.

118.

Take initiative.

If you're unclear, ask for clarification. If you can't see the front board, change seats. The point is, don't suffer in silence.

119. Give documents meaningful file names.

This is just another way to show consideration. For example, your advisers and professors get a lot of documents called "résumé" or "research paper." If you want yours to stand out and not get lost, include your own name in the file name (e.g., "Resume – Juan Gomez)."

120. Look for professors with a passion and skill for teaching, a strong knowledge of their subject matter, and a desire to help students succeed.

121. Pace yourself, especially on large assignments.

122. Handle the tedious parts of a paper first (e.g., the bibliography), while you still have high energy. It'll make finishing your paper that much easier and less stressful.

123. Do you know about the app called Easy Bib? It takes a lot of the tedium out of creating a bibliography. Check it out.

124. Before you sign up for Highlights of Astronomy, read the course description carefully. Maybe run it by a lawyer.

How do you bomb a test in "Highlights of Astronomy"?

I don't know, but apparently it's one of my spiritual gifts. On this, my first college midterm, I scored a whopping 24%.

Can you believe that? Twenty-five multiple-choice questions, nineteen of which I had flubbed.

Meanwhile, I was kicking ass in Latin—Latin II, for cryin' out loud. I was even learning to hold my own in Alan Shapiro's poetry class, with all those ultra-sophisticated sophomores and juniors.

But none of that even registered when the TA handed back my exam (carefully avoiding eye contact), and there at the top of the page sat a lone, spindly "6."

Six. That's only six more than you got, and you weren't even there. You probably weren't even born.

The tests had been handed back on a Friday—but since I had blithely skipped class so I could go home for the weekend, I picked up my exam the following Monday.

Clueless. It's one of the few times in my life I've been clueless about being clueless.

Later that afternoon, I ran into a guy from class—Drake, who lived in my dorm and whose real name isn't Drake. What a relief to have another freshman to commiserate with.

Drake had done okay. Not great, but okay. I was careful not to tip my hand, only to say the exam had not gone well. With no trace of a smile, Drake looked me in the eye and asked, "You're not that *six* he was talking about, are you?"

I'm pretty sure I lied.

By the time I reached my room, I was crying and practically wheezing. I crammed every book I could into my JanSport backpack, strapped it on, and made a penitential run for the library.

Out the door and barely onto the quad, I ran into Vince Gerasole, who was walking in the opposite direction. Vince was a senior. He had sort of a Billy Joel vibe. He saw my sobs and asked with big-brotherly concern, "What's wrong?"

Through my tears, I choked out the story of how I had flunked the Highlights of Astronomy midterm, and how I was now off to the library. *Or the convent.*

Vince put his foot down. "You're not going to the library," he said. "C'mon. We're going to J.K. Sweets."

It was so Greg Brady (to my Jan), but that's what I needed. Vince was a good student with a bright future. In that moment, I was neither. So his faith in me felt like an encounter with an angel. Maybe it was.

I should also mention that in the early 1980s, J.K. Sweets was as good as the gettin' got. In both my years at Northwestern, this is the most fun I would ever have on a Monday—which I'm sure says more about me than it does about Northwestern.

Vince and I walked the block or two to J.K. Sweets, where he grabbed a table for two. I still felt deflated and sniffly—and though I tried not to show it, I'm sure my posture gave me away.

As we sat quietly eating our ice cream with little plastic spoons, Vince kept reassuring me, "*Lots* of people flunk midterms." *All-righty.*

I'll tell you what helped even more than the pep talk: remembering that John Rompon, my trusty RA, was also in Astronomy.

John was a double major whose GPA was somewhere in the stratosphere. Even *he* thought

Highlights of Astronomy felt like Advanced Astrophysics. So much so that one afternoon he knocked on my open door and said solemnly, "Let's meet with the dean."

I didn't know what a dean was, but with John in charge, who cared? We were going to do something about this outrage, and we were going to do it together. I could not have been more down with the plan if it had come with Paul McCartney tickets.

Our mission was clear: to call out Highlights of Astronomy for what it was—something far beyond the survey course it purported to be—and to get our course status changed from a letter grade to a pass/fail.

(I didn't even know you could take a class pass/fail. See? All the more reason to have at least one college senior in your corner.)

If Vince Gerasole had a Billy Joel vibe, John Rompon had a John Rompon vibe. I used to tease him about his signature strut. John didn't just exude confidence—he awakened the confidence in everyone around him.

John had also just been named to homecoming court, which should not have mattered, but somehow helped. Any way you looked at it, John's credibility soared above mine. He was as outraged by his B as I was hankering for one.[4]

Together, on a snowy Friday morning, John and I met with the dean, and just to show I meant business, I wore high heels. Too bad I also wore jeans. I'm sure the suits in the dean's suite were quaking in their wing tips as I made my tottering entrance.

I took my seat next to John, and for obvious reasons, let him do most of the talking.

The dean was cordial, but noncommittal. Still, John and I left the man's office with our heads held high and our fingers crossed. Back at the

4. I don't recall John's midterm grade. I do know he ended up with no less than a B in the course. But I'm getting ahead of myself.

dorm, I could not change out of those high heels fast enough.

One late afternoon about a week later, John showed up again at my door. He was wearing his big bright-orange down jacket, and his cheeks were red.

"John, you're beaming like a Christmas tree!" By now it practically *was* Christmas.

"I just came from the dean's office," he said. "They granted our request!"

YES. High tens, hugs, and a tidal wave of relief. Not since being intercepted by Vince Gerasole on the way to the library had I felt so full of hope. Now all I had to do was squeak through Highlights of Astronomy with a passing grade.

I did. I honestly couldn't tell you how. It wasn't pretty, I remember that much. But thanks be to God, not everything in life has to be pretty. Sometimes a passing grade is all we need. That, and a little help from our friends.

Special thanks to Vince Gerasole and John Rompon for their roles in this story—and for letting me share it.

125. Don't assume a course with no prerequisites is going to be a slam dunk.

126. Don't assume you can pass a pass/fail course with a D+. I'm pretty sure *that* perk disappeared around the time Reagan left office.

127. Find out the last day for receiving a hundred percent tuition refund.

Mark this day on your calendar, in case you need to/want to drop a course.

128.

Don't be afraid to drop a course.

It isn't cheating. Just do it while you still can, penalty free. Ask me if I have any regrets about dropping Greek, calculus, or Latin III.

129. Learn how to breathe deeply to calm yourself down—you'll need it for when one of your classmates decides to dominate a class discussion.

130. Don't be that student who dominates discussions.

131. Take courses outside the standard curriculum. Have fun with them.

"My biggest piece of advice for college students is to take a breadth of different courses and don't shortchange yourself by just taking classes that fit into the career you think you want.

Taking different types of courses teaches you different things about yourself and the world around you. These lessons probably won't include what is on the course syllabus, to the disappointment of your professors, but are lessons you learn along the way about yourself and how you rise to the occasion of a challenge.

For example I was a film production major and minored in business. The film classes helped bolster my creativity and gave me general technical knowledge on cameras and editing that I planned to use in a future career as a video editor.

Then there were the business classes that gave me a whole knew perspective and appreciation of what it is to work. Taking business classes challenged me to study differently and to evaluate how I learn.

The lessons in the classroom were valuable to my personal finances and helped give me confidence that I was able to do more than just work under a manager for a company; someday I could manage others or run my own company. I'm still working on that last part, but I know I have it in me to do whatever I set my mind to."

– Katie T., senior video editor and former student of mine

132. Call your professors by their proper names and titles. If you're not sure, ask respectfully, "What would you prefer your students call you?"

133. Always, I mean always, spell your professors' names correctly.

134. Don't ever think that brilliance or superior position makes up for bad behavior.

135. Buy yourself pens you like and will enjoy taking notes with. Need a recommendation? Try Pilot G-2 (medium point) gel pens.

136. It's okay to refer to yourself and your peers as kids, but start thinking of yourself as a young adult. You are a young adult.

137. Challenge yourself to write with clarity and simplicity. Don't be surprised or disillusioned if takes several drafts.

138. Show, don't tell. It's the difference between "It was a dark and stormy night" and "Thunder crashed."

139. Take some risks with your writing.

Some of the most enjoyable, most engaging reflection papers I have read included stories from the heart, song lyrics, deep thoughts, and humor. (Real humor, not bathroom humor.)

Writing is so much more rewarding when you dare to develop your unique voice. The world needs your voice.

140. Break any rule in writing, as long as you know the rule and are breaking it consciously.

141.

Spellcheck and proofread.

I know that sounds obvious, but I can't tell you how many papers/résumés I've seen with *manger* instead of *manager* and *asses* instead of *assess*.

142. Let your respect come through in your tone, as well as in your choice of words.

For example, instead of asking your professor, "Why?" (which can sound confrontational), say, "Help me understand."

143. Beware the sudden urge to deep-clean your closet right before finals.

When the pressure is on to study, sometimes we would rather do *anything* else, from deep-cleaning the closet to bathing the cat to rearranging the spice rack—or building a spice rack. I know it's hard, but remind yourself to keep your focus where it belongs.

Choosing a Major That Excites You

You know how college applications ask you to indicate your intended major? Just once, I'd like to see a checkbox for "Undecided, and Proud of It." At seventeen or eighteen, you're not supposed to know your major—you're supposed to be figuring out who you're taking to prom. Once that decision is behind you, use this section to help discern your ideal major.

144. As much as possible, let your choice of a major be your choice.

I know in some cultures, this might sound like a strange assertion—the United States is notoriously individualistic.

But if you're not comfortable with the major that's been chosen for you, I strongly encourage you to speak to a career counselor who can help you explore your options.

145. The time to ask, "What can I do with this major?" is before you declare it.

146. Choose your major based on your career aspirations—not the other way around.

147. Look beyond the "obvious" major.

Suppose you've done your research, and you're planning to pursue a career in advertising. Before declaring your major, consider other options along with advertising (e.g., marketing, psychology, or English).

As you can imagine, advertising is a broad field with various subspecialties: media buying, market research, account management, copywriting, design, and so forth. Each requires a certain background and skill set.

So let's say you're interested in copywriting. Talk to a number of copywriters and employers who hire copywriters. Ask them what fields they recommend you study.

I've met several employers who say they prefer to hire English majors over advertising majors. *Reason:* English majors (so they say) bring more breadth and depth to their writing.

148. If you're pursuing a secondary-admit program, have a backup plan.

A secondary admit program is one that requires you to apply and get accepted—even after you're admitted to the college or university. Certain majors may require a minimum GPA, or they may limit the number of students who are admitted each year.

As with so many other things, it's better to have a backup plan and not need one than to need a backup plan and not have one.

149. Make sure you're getting maximum credit for coursework completed at other colleges or universities.

It might mean walking around to different academic departments, with syllabi in hand, to show how Course A at the old institution corresponds to Course B at the new one. There are no guarantees, but it's still worth a try.

150. Choose a major with some versatility, in case your career plans change.

151. Before choosing a major, spend some time in the student bookstore to get a better sense of the required reading.

The required reading will either steer you toward a particular major or away from it. Just don't expect any textbook to be a page-turner.

152. Before declaring a major, take a stroll through the academic department.

You'll learn plenty just by reading the slogans, bumper stickers, and other paraphernalia on the doors of the faculty.

Also look at what sort of events the department sponsors. Are they ones you care about and identify with?

153. Forget about how awkward you might feel—arrange to sit in on a few classes.

In one day's time, you can get a quick read on the peer group, the professors, and the major you're considering.

Succeeding Beyond the Classroom

So much of your learning will happen when you're not studying, taking notes, or taking exams. (I dream of a college where none of these things are necessary.) This section will help you succeed, far beyond your transcript.

154.

Take weekends to **recharge**, not simply to escape.

155. For an excellent read on how mentors can help you succeed in college and afterward, look up Thomas P. Friedman's excellent article, "It Takes a Mentor" (New York Times, Sept. 9, 2014).

156. Take advantage of events that come to campus, and student organizations where you can develop your skills and make friends for a lifetime.

"My main regret of my college experience is that I did not participate in extracurricular activities. I have never been sporty and sororities weren't for me, but I realize now that serving on a committee of some sort, or applying for an honors society would have given me an edge on my résumé and a stronger sense of community within my alma mater. I now realize that I would have found active participation or leadership in an interest group as a fun AND educational part of college."

– Lindsay D., recent college graduate

157. Ask yourself, "Is what I'm doing the best use of my time?" If it isn't, figure out what is and do that instead.

158. If the spirit moves you, get involved on campus as early as possible.

"My biggest piece of advice for college students would be to get involved on campus, and get involved early. Joining clubs, a Greek organization, a sports team, academic groups, or anything else your campus offers can add so much to your college experience!

Sure, everyone knows the excuse everyone gives (especially their first semester): 'I need time to transition to college and focus on my studies.' Well, speaking as someone who was the head of a recruiting organization on campus, I can confidently say that in the vast majority of cases, joining a group your first semester on campus greatly aids in your transition from high school to college.

You get to meet new people (and in many cases people who are or have taken the same classes you are taking), which helps tremendously when you're starting out. By adding group activities to your schedule, you learn how to better manage and prioritize your time. If you're looking for a more tangible reason to be active on campus, it's this: The experiences and possible leadership opportunities that campus organizations can offer will help you develop skills that will set you apart in an interview for your first job after graduation.

During my interviews after graduation, I talked more about my campus organization experience than my coursework. I believe that without that experience, I would not have the position I have today. If I wasn't involved on campus, I would not have made the lifelong friendships that I hold so dear, I would not have the fond memories of experiences that were unique to that organization, and most of all ... I would not be the person I am today."

– Jeff G., young MBA and full-time management consultant

159. Protect yourself. Life should be fair, but as of this writing, it isn't.

For example, you should be able to walk home alone at eleven o'clock at night, with no threat to your safety. In reality, I wouldn't recommend it. There's only one you.

For more specific tips and resources, check your college's campus safety department.

160. Read Gavin de Becker's book, *The Gift of Fear: Survival Signals That Protect Us From Violence.*

161. Get as much exposure as you can, as early as you can, to career fields that interest you.

"Get a job working in your chosen field as early as possible; e.g., if you want to be a CPA, work in the office of a CPA firm doing something, anything, as early as possible.

The younger you are, the easier your chances. Don't wait until everything is perfect, you've passed your CPA exam, you have your degree, and then find out you don't like the field or can't land a job."

– Joe B., CPA/hiring manager

162. Even if you consider yourself to be shy, get some experience during college working with the public. It'll serve you well in your personal and professional life.

163. Don't feel obligated to lend anyone your car, money, or textbook.

And don't be offended if someone doesn't want to lend you theirs.

164.

Communicate.

For example, why can't linen companies just come right out and say, "The tag on the fitted sheet goes on the top left corner of your mattress"?

Now you know. If you think you might forget, take a permanent pen and write "Top left corner" on the tag. You'll be glad you did.

165. Be thankful for your roommates.

They're there to remind you that not every family is as nutty as your own—some are much more so.

166. Do private things in private.

167. Have a friendly way of getting rid of Camping Carl.

When someone wanders into your room or work space and won't leave, try standing up, gracefully walking Carl to the door, and saying cheerfully, "Gotta go!" If it's someone you know and like, you can also use my father's line: "Thanks for coming over last night!"

168. Clean up after yourself, especially in common areas, like the dorm bathroom.

169. Use the Paperless (iPhone) app to keep lists and get more done.

170. Challenge yourself to drop the filler phrases (e.g., like, you know) from your speech.

171. Try not to end statements with an upward inflection—it will make you sound unsure of yourself. For example, instead of saying, "I went to class today?" say, "I went to class today."

172. Don't correct other people when it really isn't necessary.

173. Get together with friends and sing along to the guitar, loudly, and as often as possible. Preferably not when others are trying to sleep.

174.

Carry yourself with confidence.

More specifically, when you meet someone for the first time, smile, stand up straight, make eye contact, and offer a sincere handshake.

I knew a hiring manager who used to say when a candidate slouched or cowered, it sent the message, "You don't want to hire me, do you?" And his internal response would always be, *No, I don't.* Let that be someone else's style, but not yours.

175. Make your own travel reservations. It will add to your confidence and reinforce your status as a young adult.

176. Before giving or taking advice, consider who lives with the consequences.

177. Don't hate me because I'm not a vegetarian. We're all drawn to different causes.

178. If you get summoned for jury duty, go.

You'll learn more about group dynamics and our judicial system than you would from a whole semester of Sociology or Political Science.

Just be sure to take your iPad and a charger. Comfortable shoes are also a must, especially if you have to park in another ZIP code. Last time I was called, I even brought an inflatable seat cushion. Jury duty involves a lot of sitting.

179. Use self-insight as a springboard to change, not as an excuse to stay stuck.

180. Figure out what motivates you, and your life will never be the same.

One of the keys to a fulfilling life is to identify your favorite skills and outcomes, and let them come out to play—even when your aspirations sound almost kindergarten simple.

A few examples:

- "I just want to nurture and care for others." (a nurse/my cousin Jeanne)
- "I like to draw pictures." (an art director/ former co-worker; the same guy who said, "I don't want to say grace over a plate of nachos.")
- "I want to affirm and encourage other people." (yours truly)

What do *you* want to do? What is it you can't *not* do?

Don't worry for now how it sounds. Later, if you have to, you can translate your aspirations into language that clicks with a potential employer or customer.

181. Write down what *doesn't* motivate you. It'll help you clarify what does.

Try this: Fold a blank sheet of paper in half, lengthwise. In the left column, write down all the things about your past or present jobs you've *not* enjoyed; e.g., dealing with screaming kids, working under constant pressure, or feeling stuck behind a desk.

In the right column, next to each item, write down what you prefer instead. For example, you might enjoy working with kids, but prefer an environment where they're not screaming—a school, for example, as opposed to a restaurant.

Use your list to identify opportunities that would be a good fit for you.

182. Focus on your preferred *outcomes,* not just your favorite skills.

You would think using your favorite skills would lead automatically to career bliss—and for a while, it does.

Here's an example: I knew from an early age that one of my gifts was writing. And I was fortunate after college to earn a full-time paycheck from that gift, first as a copywriter, then as an editor (my friends used to call me "Slash").

But after fourteen years, I grew tired of writing phrases like *performance metrics* and *perfect for today's active lifestyles.* The kicker came when one of my freelance clients told me, "You just need to get a *real* job and come work for us."

Yeah, no.

Truth be told, I was and am still grateful for those years. They brought me not only a paycheck, but valuable lessons and lifelong friends.

But it turns out the real motivation for me is not so much writing (which I love) as inspiring people to laugh, lighten up, and live their best life. Writing is just a means toward that end.

Moral of the story: Apply the skills you love toward whatever outcomes light you up. Nearly every workday will then feel like play. And the days that don't? They're the reasons we get paid.

183. Informational interviews, my friend. Informational interviews.

If you really want to find out what it's like to work in a particular job or industry, there's no substitute for meeting face-to-face with those who are already there. That, in a nutshell, is what informational interviewing is all about.

Free online bonus: Download the article "How to Conduct Informational Interviews Like a Pro" at ultimatereminders.com/free-college-downloads.

184. Leave at your peak, and leave on good terms, even with those you find difficult. Life is too short and the world is too small to leave bad tracks.

185. Take the Myers-Briggs—it can help you understand how you're wired and what you need to do your best work.

In case you're not familiar with it, the Myers-Briggs Type Indicator (MBTI) is a commonly used personality assessment. Among other things, it can give you insight into your personality strengths and challenges.

The MBTI takes less than an hour, and it's usually available for a small charge through your campus career center.

Typically, you take the assessment online, and schedule a follow-up appointment with a trained professional to go over your results.

The best counselors guide, but also encourage you to draw your own conclusions.

Like any other assessment, the Myers-Briggs has its limitations. Some psychologists put it right up there with horoscopes and fortune cookies.

Take the Myers-Briggs anyway.

You can always refute what it says, but you might find some of it useful and spot-on. I did. And the last time I had my students take the Myers-Briggs, I heard one student tell another, "This was so worth the sixteen bucks."

186. If you want to stay home and raise a family, honor that.

But finish your education. You would be hard-pressed to meet anyone who, having made this decision, later regretted it.

Completing your degree will give you a sense of accomplishment. Having an education will expand your mind, and allow you to expand the minds of your children.

And though you might not be ready to hear this, you just can't assume that someone will always be there to provide for you. Life happens. All the more reason to build a strong educational foundation.

187. Be a good roommate.

The same qualities that make for good roommates make for good co-workers.

188. Call it for what it is. If it's a party, don't call it a get-together. If it's a dorm, don't call it a living center.

189. Don't show up to the party just as everyone else is leaving.

190. Before joining a fraternity or sorority, weigh the time commitment.

191.

Get beyond your coursework.

For example, if you're an art major, venture out to a few exhibits. If you're a Spanish major, immerse yourself in a Spanish-speaking culture.

192. Before requesting another roommate, do your best to work things out with the one you've got—unless you're concerned about your sanity, your safety, or the safety of your belongings.

193. Try not to talk more *about* your roommate than you do *to* your roommate.

If the two of you aren't getting along, you can always ask for guidance from your RA—but whenever possible, work it out directly.

194. Show your roommate respect, even if you're not feeling it. That's how you maintain self-respect.

195. If your roommate brings dangerous or toxic people into your room (or toxic/illegal substances), that's your cue to petition for a room change.

196. Have a life separate from your roommate, even if he or she is the greatest person in the world.

197. Get to know your alumni association, even before you graduate. They want to help you succeed, both during college and long after.

Internships and Careers

As a career counselor, I could (and probably should) write a whole book on this subject. For now, the tips in this section should make for a good, healthy start.

P.S. The sooner you start, the more options you will have.

198. Take another deep breath.

You don't have to figure out the rest of your life. You only have to decide your next move.

199. If you can afford to do an unpaid internship, and the experience is worthwhile, do it.

You'll gain firsthand industry exposure, valuable new contacts, and professional credibility—all of which will serve you long after the internship ends.

Just ask Katie T., the former student of mine who was quoted in #131.

The summer after her sophomore year, Katie began a full-time internship with the Palace of Auburn Hills, near Detroit. By the time it was over, only two out of the five original interns were still standing—Katie was one of them. The others had either quit or been dismissed.

But the end of the internship wasn't the end of the

story. As Katie described it to me at the time in an email:

"I've been working for NBA TV as a runner (a paid position) during the NBA finals. It has been the experience of a lifetime. Who knew the Pistons would go all the way?!?! After Game Three on Thursday I was in their locker room with the camera crew, waiting for them to finish the tape they were recording on. I got to see all the Pistons players up close and personal! Tonight I'll be in the Lakers' locker room! I've also been able to meet a lot of different broadcasters and production crew from L.A., New York, New Jersey, and everywhere in between. It's really exciting and a lot of fun."

200. Look for internship benefits that are high-value to you and low-cost to your internship site.

Examples: Weekly mentoring and exposure to other areas of interest within the organization. Job-shadowing. The chance to contribute to important projects. And at least one strong letter of reference upon completing the internship successfully.

201. Don't confuse a stipend with a wage.

If your internship pays only a stipend, don't torture yourself by calculating what you're "making" hourly—focus instead on what you can gain from the experience.

202. See internships as a chance to try before you buy.

The ideal internship lets you experience a particular profession *before* you commit to it. It's either going to confirm your career hunches or start to talk you out of them. Either way, it's good information.

203. Be thankful that internships have a built-in shelf life. Most of them last no more than a summer or a semester. Which means if it doesn't work out, you're not locked in.

204. Don't pass up a good internship because it requires you to pay for credits.

Of course it's ironic to have to pay for the privilege of working for free. As a former intern, I've lived that irony at least three times. (But I'm not bitter.)

In fact, those same internships opened up a brand-new world to me; namely, that of helping college students plan their careers. I also realized a college campus is much more laid back than a business environment—and to my surprise, I liked that.

Long story short, those unpaid internships changed everything. They also allowed me to graduate with my dream job: university career counselor.

Once I was in that job and working with student interns, I saw the whole dynamic from another angle. It turns out both students and internship sites benefit when the university can be involved, and whenever necessary, hold each side accountable.

205. If your internship site isn't delivering as promised, try resolving the issue directly. If that doesn't work, ask a professor or adviser to get involved. That's part of what you're paying for.

206. Unless an internship is off-the-charts heinous, tough it out.

If you do, you won't have to explain to a future employer why it ended. You will also be establishing yourself as someone who keeps commitments.

On the other hand, I am not for a moment suggesting you put up with abuse or exploitation. When in doubt about what to do, talk to a trusted mentor.

207. Treat every internship like one long job interview. More often than not, that's exactly what it is.

208. Before moving to a new city, consider lining up an internship so you can see what it would be like to live and work there, longer term.

209. Don't shy away from a job offer just because it comes to you without a lot of struggle.

This is especially true if the offer comes through an internship. Employers use internship programs as a recruiting tool. So if they offer you a job, they're *hoping* you accept it.

210. Before you call yourself a go-getter, make sure you can back it up with examples.

211. Use job-market trends to confirm a career choice, not to make one.

If you focus too much on the fastest growing careers, without regard for your skills and motivations, you could find yourself supremely disappointed—likewise for the people you serve. (Ever gotten a shot from a nurse who hated her work? I don't recommend it.)

Better to find the sweet spot between what you want to do, what you're good at, and what will pay the bills.

Incidentally, you can find a wealth of free information in the U.S. Department of Labor's Occupational Outlook Handbook (www.bls.gov/ooh).

212.

Invest in yourself.

This is no time to settle for a cheap suit, a bad haircut, or a lackluster résumé. This, from one who has seen all three.

213. Start writing down your STAR stories.

Whenever you interview for jobs, internships, or even volunteer roles, you'll probably get questions along the lines of, "Tell me about a time you (dealt with conflict, took initiative, went above and beyond the call of duty, etc.)."

These behavioral questions assume that how you've dealt with situations in the past indicates how you would deal with them in the future.

The STAR acronym gives you an easy, effective way to frame your answers. Here's what it looks like:

S: Describe the **situation** you were faced with.

T: Identify the **task** at hand.

A: Specify the **action** you took to address the situation.

R: Share the **results** or outcomes you achieved.

Here's an example of a STAR story on initiative and innovation.

The career center where I worked went from having too few student appointments to having too many. This made it difficult for students with urgent needs to see us in a timely fashion. (Situation)

One of my co-workers and I realized the problem could be alleviated by requiring all students with résumé questions to attend a brief workshop on résumé basics before coming in for one-on-one appointments. We pitched the idea to our supervisor who told us, "Make it happen." (Task)

We did. We created a simple workshop that could be used by the entire office. We also collaborated with the office manager to offer the workshop at various times/locations that would be convenient to students' schedules. (Action)

Almost immediately, our calendars opened up, allowing us to help more students in less time. We improved not only our efficiency, but also our rapport and reputation with students. (Results)

214.

Distinguish between a passion and a pastime.

In the words of the late George Balanchine, the famous ballet director, "I don't hire people who 'want' to dance. I hire people who *have* to dance."

What is it you have to do?

Career or Calling?

Okay. It's impossible for me to talk about a calling without referencing the One who calls. As always, filter what I've written through the lens of your own beliefs, and apply only what you find helpful.

Career	Calling
Self-chosen; you find it	God-chosen; it finds you
100% self-directed	Carried out with Christ and for Christ
Driven by "where the jobs are"	Driven by the best use of your gifts
Drains your energy	Lights you up
Can compromise other important values/commitments	Expresses your values; nourishes other key commitments
Primary rewards: money, status, power, prestige, pleasure	Primary rewards: joy, peace, sense of contribution/fulfillment
"What's in it for me?"	"How may I serve?"
Self is glorified, sometimes at others' expense	God is glorified, to the enrichment of others and self
Highest reward: Make your mark in history.	Highest reward: Make your mark on Eternity.

215. Remember that your résumé and cover letter don't need to get you the job—they only need to get you an interview.

216. Unless you're delivering your résumé in person, include a cover letter.

A compelling cover letter is your opportunity to connect with the prospective employer, bring your résumé to life, and ask for the next step; namely, an interview.

217. Use a professional-sounding email address.

Not dizzylizzy@ ... Not whosyourdaddy ... Not devilsmistress ... This is especially key when communicating with professors, potential employers, and anyone else in a position to help you.

218. Steer clear of résumé templates or wizards.

They're hard to work with, and while they may seem professional at first glance, to an employer they scream *generic*.

219. Have a substantive reason for choosing the major you did. It's likely to come up in an interview.

Be honest, of course, without botching your own cause.

For example, it's one thing to say you began exploring criminal justice after watching your favorite crime show. But so did a lot of other people. What sustains your interest?

This is the time to talk about meaningful class projects, job shadows, internships, conferences you've attended, and any other direct involvement. How do you see yourself contributing to your field? These are all good points to be able to articulate.

220. "Filter everything through, *I am a professional.*"[5]

This simple affirmation will affect your smile, your eye contact, your handshake, your hygiene, how you dress, and everything else about how you conduct yourself.

221. Figure out your must-haves.

If you did the exercise in #181, you have a growing sense of your ideal work conditions. Go through your finished list, and mark the items that matter most to you—the things that would make the greatest difference in your accepting a job or not.

When we're first starting out, we're probably not going to get everything we want. But you should be able to get *some* things on your list. The point is, it's much easier to hit a target you've taken time to define.

5. This is a direct quote from John Challenger of Challenger, Gray & Christmas, whom I once interviewed for an employment article.

222. Look at the job vacancy through the eyes of the prospective employer.

"I have three basic rules that govern my hiring practice: (1) Can you do the job? (2) Will you do the job? (3) Do you fit into the company/organizational culture?

I have found many people who were exceptional at one and two. Number three is much more difficult. Imagine someone free-spirited working for a biological laboratory. Not such a good fit."

– Ellie Ramos, the grad-school classmate and hiring manager quoted in #85 and #92

223. Before the interview, get a sense of the employer's culture.

Much of this information can be found online. Whenever possible (and without being creepy), try using the employer's products and services, or talking to customers or employees.

224. Pay attention to your appearance, even for a phone interview.

You'll feel better about yourself if you dress up. It also helps to stand up and smile (for bonus points, keep a mirror handy). The added self-confidence will come through in your voice.

225. Weed out any information on your résumé that undermines your cause.

Serving as a Big Brother/Big Sister, yes. Playing Dungeons & Dragons, probably not—unless somehow that fits in with where you're applying. When in doubt, get a good second opinion.

226. Work to improve your communication skills in as many ways as possible.

Employers consistently say this is the most important skill in new college grads—and the one skill most lacking. So if you get this one right, you'll be miles ahead.

227. After every interview, send a timely and meaningful thank-you note.

I'm always sort of shocked by how few job candidates do this, especially since it's one of the fastest, easiest ways to make another favorable impression. Send it while the employer is still deciding whom to hire or call back.

When a candidate *doesn't* send a thank-you, the interviewer tends to think, "Really?" At best, it's a missed opportunity. At worst, it shows a lack of regard and a lack of job savvy. Obviously, that's not the impression you're going for.

228. Don't let anyone see you with your hands in your pockets. It just doesn't say *motivated*, *energetic*, or *professional*. To many people, it says the opposite.

229. Don't expect your college career center to find you a job—that's your job.

230. Keep private information private.

On your résumé, for example, don't include your age, marital status, diagnoses, or picture—even if you're great-looking. It's just not necessary, and it could be harmful.

231. Be advised that federal law prohibits employment discrimination based on race, color, religion, sex, or national origin. For more information, visit www.eeoc.gov.

232. Unless you're going straight into grad school, do your best to have a job lined up by the time you graduate.

233. Don't go to grad school just to escape the job market.

234. Don't lose heart if the job search takes longer than anticipated. More often than not, it does. Incidentally, two weeks is not a long time.

235. Invest as much time each week as you reasonably can toward finding meaningful work.

If you're investing only five hours per week, it's going to take you a lot longer to find a job than if you're putting in thirty hours per week.

236. Use the Internet for research, but then go meet in person with those who can hire you, recommend you, refer you, or guide you.

237. Remember that if you get the right job offer, one is all you need.

238. Once you do get an offer, get back to the employer well within the agreed-upon time frame.

Don't leave them dangling till the bitter end. You want to remind them with your words, tone, and conduct that making you the offer was a great idea for both of you.

239. My mother's best advice when choosing a profession: Make sure you're proud to be associated with those who are already in it.

240. Your online presence *is* your prospective employer's business. Proceed with caution.

241. Go to the career fair before you need a job. Dress the part. Be the part.

242. If you need a summer job or stopgap job, get one where you'll grow and/or meet people of influence.

Caddying at a country club, for example, is probably going to do you more good than bussing tables at a diner.

243. Don't assume all for-profit organizations are evil or all nonprofits are good.

244. Don't say you want to work at SeaWorld because it would be "fun."

If you want fun, buy a ticket. I tell you this not to be flippant but because working at any theme park/entertainment venue is not at all the same as attending as a guest—and I'd rather you heard it from me than from someone who can hire you.

Here's what to talk about instead: the overlap between the employer's needs and your interests.

For example, one of my former co-workers who *did* interview with SeaWorld spoke about her passion for arts education. They hired her. She later found out she was the only candidate who *did not* say she thought working at SeaWorld would be "fun."

245. If you're not sure how to tie a tie, visit tie-a-tie.net.

246. Have a solid answer for why you're interested in this particular employer, and why this department or division.

For example, if you're interviewing with the XYZ Company marketing department, make sure you can articulate why you're interested in XYZ—and why the marketing department.

247. Speak in terms of the employer's interests, not simply your own.

I can't tell you how many candidates I've interviewed who said they wanted this job because they needed benefits. The employer wants to know how you'll *contribute.*

248. If you're *not* jazzed about a particular position, don't fake it. On the other hand, stay upbeat and professional.

249.

Don't go into an interview without first having done a practice interview.

Practice interviews give us courage, confidence, and a much-needed reality check. They let us work out the verbal and nonverbal kinks while we still can, and before there are consequences.

250. In job interviews, tell *and* show. Be ready to back up your claims with examples.

251. Connect the dots so the employer doesn't have to.

Whenever you're writing or speaking to a prospective employer, show how your background relates, and how it adds value. Don't assume the employer will take time to draw the connection.

252. Polish your shoes, especially before an important meeting or interview.

253. Err on the side of overpreparing for interviews.

I have never interviewed a candidate who was too prepared. But I've met countless candidates who were woefully *under*prepared. Don't let that be you.

254. Don't say you want this job or internship because you like working with people.

Focus instead on the industry, and the contributions you will make.

When I was a senior in college, I heard a career consultant named Marilyn Moats Kennedy say, "If you like working with people, you haven't worked with enough of them."

255. Have a good answer for the inevitable "weakness" question.

Some downright *bad* answers:

"I'm a perfectionist."
"I'm too nice."
"I work too hard."
"I hit people."
"I oversleep."

The first three answers are overused, and the next two more or less scream *deal-breaker*. As does the worst answer of all: "I don't have any weaknesses."

Everyone has weaknesses. The employer wants to know you're self-aware enough to admit them and disciplined enough to keep them in check. The best weaknesses are surmountable, not mission critical, and under your control.

Need an example? Okay. Here's how I might answer the weakness question.

Patience doesn't always come naturally, so I have to go out of my way to make it happen. I can tell you I have a healthy sense of urgency, and I know how to get things done to a high standard. My bosses and co-workers have always appreciated my habit of meeting deadlines cheerfully, without being reminded.

256. In any interview, formal or informal, don't answer the "weakness" question before you're asked.

Job interviews require integrity, but they don't require you to botch your own cause—like the student who let me know right up front (thankfully, in a practice interview) that his GPA was not the best.

I pointed out politely that his GPA was already on his résumé, and he would not have been scheduled for an interview had the prospective employer found his grades unacceptable.

And I don't mean to pick on one student. Lots of people, in an effort to be modest, jump ahead to the weakness question. I'm asking you not to be one of them.

257. If a prospective employer takes you to lunch or dinner, recognize you're still being interviewed. Be friendly, but stay in interview mode.

258. If your campus offers an etiquette lunch or dinner, sign up, clean up, dress up, and go.

The experience will add to your knowledge and comfort level—and the food is usually amazing.

259. Conduct yourself in such a way that your co-workers will miss you when you're gone and want to see you back.

260. Don't be caught yawning on the job, or even on breaks. Again, it just doesn't say *professional.*

261. If you're going to travel right after you graduate, start planting the seeds of your job search long before you go. Also have a plan for how you're going to gear up again once you get back home.

FRIENDS, FAMILY, AND FAMBLY[6]

So much of your happiness will hinge not on your accomplishments but on how you treat other people—and how you let them treat you.

This section will help you cultivate relationships that are mutually nourishing and otherwise uplifting. You truly don't have time for anything less.

6. How do you define *fambly*? Though Steinbeck might not agree, I think of fambly as any friend who feels like family and any family member who is also a friend.

262. Now that you're in college, treat your parents with more respect, not less.

Respect their time, property, and opinions, even if you disagree. As the saying goes, "Learn how to disagree without being disagreeable." That's one of the best ways to show respect.

263. Don't be too quick to label other people, especially your family.

Save words like "abusive" and "dysfunctional" for situations that truly call for that. Much of what gets labeled *dysfunctional* is simply human imperfection.

Incidentally, any family that claims to have *no* issues probably has more issues than your family and mine put together.

264.

Don't be too quick to label yourself.

Do you really have Obsessive-Compulsive Disorder (OCD), or do you just like using a paper towel on public doorknobs? There's a world of difference.

Here's the problem with using loaded words carelessly: We exaggerate our own plight while trivializing someone else's.

265. Go ahead. Poke fun at your loved ones when they misuse the word "literally."

As in, "John. Literally. Went. *Bananas.*"

(a direct quote from my dad, whose latest hijinks somehow involved my brother John)

How do you "literally" go bananas??

266. Write down the classic, offbeat things your family members say in everyday conversation. Months or years later, you'll be glad you did.

267. Don't become anyone's counselor unless you're licensed and getting paid for it.

Particularly when you get to college, you're going to meet people who have problems greater than your capacity to solve or listen to. That's why we have counselors, psychologists, ministers, and rabbis—they're *trained* to handle crises.

268. Pay attention to how you feel around those you call your friends.

Do you feel diminished? Uplifted? Drained? Supported?

Be honest. The friendships that are right for you will grow stronger under such scrutiny. The friendships that aren't so healthy might need to be scaled back or eliminated.

As I've said before, you need and deserve healthy relationships—but it's up to you to make them happen.

269. Don't get enmeshed with someone else's problems at the expense of dealing with your own.

Sometimes focusing on other people's drama is easier, but it's definitely not smart. You've got your own responsibilities—and only you can deal with them. Beware the friend or loved one who tries to convince you otherwise.

270. Anytime you're struggling continuously, reach out for help.

It doesn't mean you're weak. On the contrary, it probably means you're wise and brave.

Start with the resources on your own campus—tutoring, academic advising, counseling, career advising, and so on.

And if you run into brick walls or bad advice, keep looking. You may have to go through several counselors, for example, to find one you like and who can help you. It's normal. Knowing this can keep you from giving up too soon.

271. Make the kind of friends in college you'll want to have thirty years from now—and of course, be that kind of friend.

272.

Be a friend, but not a martyr.

Once when I started to take on a friend's suffering (thinking I was being helpful), my friend said very nicely, "Ah, don't internalize my bullsh*t."

273. When one of your friends needs more help than you can give, offer to walk with him or her to the campus counseling office—and/or meet up afterward.

274. Beware the psychedelic drug that goes by the street name "Gaga."

In more old-fashioned circles, it's called infatuation. Who hasn't been infatuated to the point of delusion? It's that old Dierks Bentley song, "What Was I Thinkin'."

I know what it is to compromise sacred values because he's cute, he's hilarious, he thinks you're hilarious (and cute), and what are the odds that you would both love oxygen?

Go slow. As I said in *Ultimate Reminders for Everyday Life,* "Don't get serious with someone who's been in your life less time than the box of baking soda."

275. Trust that if a relationship is meant to last longer and grow stronger, it will.

In the meantime, surround yourself with friends who can tell you what you need to hear, not just what you want to hear.

276. When the Good Lord pulls you from a burning building, don't go back in.

Likewise for running back in, crawling back in, or drifting back in. Too often, that's exactly what we do. We give endless chances to situations and people who have already shown themselves to be no good for us.

Better simply to move on. Don't even do a drive-by.

277.

Listen to those who love you the most.

Once, when I was getting over a guy, my mother told me, "The friend you're looking for might not be the life of the party—he might not even be at the party."

My father was more direct: "You want me to kick his ass?"

278. Beware the person you love but just don't like.

279. Beware the person you like but don't respect.

280. Respect yourself.

281. Pay attention to how other people get attention.

Are they loud? Funny? Dramatic? Helpful? Figure out which behaviors you want to encourage, and which ones you don't. What gets rewarded gets repeated.

282. Pay attention to how *you* get attention.

By being loud? Funny? Dramatic? Helpful? Decide how you would like to be known, and what kind of people you would like to attract. Then as best you can, conduct yourself accordingly.

283. When you meet someone whose constant vibe is, "If only the world were as perceptive and humble as I am," *run*. Martyr complexes wear thin faster than cheap undies.

284. Try not to buy cheap undies. Better to buy the good ones on sale.

285. Don't try to unscramble an egg. Steer clear of situations where you'll wish you could.

286. You're going to have friends who don't go to college. Don't treat them less than, and don't let them treat *you* less than.

287.

Hold your head high during and after a breakup.

We live with other people's behavior temporarily—we live with our own much longer. Knowing this makes it easier to take the high road, even when the other person doesn't deserve it.

288. Stay true to your friends, family, and principles. Not necessarily in that order.

289. Whenever you're visiting someone else's home, dress up a little.

At the very least, aim for "snappy casual." This is especially true when it's a holiday meal or other special occasion. Once you're home, you can change back into jeans or yoga pants.

290. Resist the temptation to cement new relationships by spilling your guts. New relationships need time.

291. Beware the quasi-stranger who spills *their* guts. The relationship that starts too quickly can also end too quickly—or depending on the relationship, not quickly enough.

292. Stick with the friends who bring out your best, not your worst.

293. Beware the boyfriend or girlfriend who should appeal to you but doesn't.

294. Never speak ill of your significant other's family. What we say about other people reflects on us.

295. Remember that you do marry the family.

296. Beware the person who claims to have *no* baggage.

Anyone I've ever met in this category has ended up having baggage Freud couldn't unload.

297. Don't think you'll be the one who makes him (or her) act differently.

298. Know the difference between playing hard to get and being hard to get, by virtue of your full and happy life.

299. Invest in other people who want to be invested in and who are actively investing in themselves.

300. Recognize when you leave home, you're not the only one who grows and changes. Hold a space for other people's growth as well as your own.

301. Honor the difference between a friendship and a dependency.

302. Don't be the rebound.

303. Don't make someone else *your* rebound. It's not fair.

304. Let your relationships keep pace with the person you're becoming.

As someone put it to me years ago, as you grow and change, some relationships will grow deeper, some will fall by the wayside, and new relationships will be based on your new and higher plateau.

305. Call other people, including your peers, by their preferred names.

If you're not sure what they want you to call them, ask.

306. As a friend of mine says, "Don't act like one of the girls until you know you are one."

307.

Call or text your loved ones to let them know you've arrived safely.

308. Let your parents do things for you now and then, even if you can do them yourself.

Sure, it's in giving that we receive. But sometimes it's in receiving that we give.

309. Don't send graduation announcements to people who barely know you. It can easily come across as holding out your hand for money, even if you don't intend it that way.

310. Don't skewer your parents for not being as socially correct or up with the times as you are. They came of age in a different era.

311. Remember that every generation has its virtues and blind spots—including yours, including mine.

312.

Resist the all-too-human tendency to blame your parents.

You don't have to love everything they did (or continue to do), but you do have to find a healthy way to move past it.

Good Old-Fashioned Self-Care

The point here is simple: No one can take care of you like you can take care of yourself. Get the sleep you need, get the fun you need, get the "alone" time you need. Do these things not at the expense of your other commitments, but in service of your other commitments.

313. If you feel you can't go on, stop reading and call the National Suicide Prevention Lifeline. In the U.S., their number is 1-800-273-8255.

314. Have rituals that sustain you and pull you back on track. A few examples:

- Writing in a journal
- Sitting down to a hot meal
- Exercising
- Praying
- Meditating

Rituals don't have to be deep or serious to be meaningful. If bowling does it for you, take time regularly to go bowling.

315.

Drink more **water** and less caffeine.

Your skin will look better, and you'll have more energy. It's impossible to feel your energetic best when you're dehydrated.

316. Do what it takes to have a clear complexion. Few of us feel terrific about ourselves when fighting a losing battle with breakouts.

317. Get your sleep. If necessary, set an alarm for when you should go to bed. Sleep deprivation only *sounds* fun.

318. Remember that sleep quality counts as much as quantity.

Sleeping from 11:00 p.m. to 7:00 a.m. is a lot more restful than sleeping from 3:00 a.m. to 11:00 a.m. Not nearly as much fun, but definitely more restful.

319. If you think you have the flu or something worse, see a doctor right away. The sooner you get treated, the greater your options.

320. Don't drink more alcohol on a plane than you would want your pilot to be drinking.[7]

321. Unless you're too sick to move, shower every day.

322. Give yourself the gift of time: time to get to class, and time to wind down after class.

323. Give yourself the gift of structure and a routine.

For example, having regular mealtimes and even regular study times. It'll save you the agony of having to recommit to studying each and every night, because the decision has already been made.

7. For an eye-opening look at the effects, Google the phrase *FAA Alcohol and Flying.*

324. If you give yourself a late-night manicure, expect to wake up with 300-thread-count fingernails. It's pretty awesome, unless you're going out somewhere.

325. **Have a playlist to cheer yourself up.**

326. Save your back and buy luggage with wheels.

327. Go easy on the makeup. Less truly is more.

328. If you can't have a fireplace, get a DVD of a fireplace.

329. Don't expect pills or supplements to compensate for poor health habits.

330. Whenever you need a boost, go take a brisk walk. You'll feel so much better for the rest of the day.

Even a five-minute walk can clear your mind and re-energize your whole morning. If it can work for me in a smoky Vegas hotel-casino, it can work for you, too. Naturally, a "real" workout is even better.

331. Don't wait until all conditions are perfect before you exercise. Do what you can, as often as you can.

332. In case you haven't yet learned this firsthand, a little of Vegas goes a long way.

333. Use the free app Fooducate to make better, healthier food choices.

Fooducate lets you scan the barcode of a particular food and instantly receive the food's letter grade, along with explanations and alternatives. As an example, Campbell's Tomato Soup scores a B+.

334. Unify your look. Don't be that guy in a nice suit with a mullet.

PART 3
One Foot Out.

Remember how you felt moving from high school to college? Now you're starting to plan for your next adventure after college—career, grad school, volunteer work, travel, or some combination of these.

If college has taught you anything, it's how to adapt to change. Good thing, because we'll all be learning that lesson for the rest of our lives.

Seeing the World Through New Eyes

Ever have a moment that forever alters your worldview? Years ago, I attended a panel discussion on what it was like to be a student of color on a predominantly white campus.

The subject matter was hardly new to me; I had been asking students of color about their experiences for years.

But this day, a student panelist nearly knocked me out of my chair when she thundered into the microphone, "College is meant to *prepare* students for the real world. This campus *shelters* students from the real world." *Boom!*

Will you let your campus shelter you—or prepare you?

335. Get to know people who don't look like you or think like you.

As a starting point, check out Mellody Hobson's TED Talk "Color blind or color brave?" It makes a compelling case for having difficult conversations about race, in a spirit of courage, self-awareness, and respect.

336. To get a deeper understanding of racism in the United States, watch the documentary *The Color of Fear*.

Despite being filmed in 1993, *The Color of Fear* is still relevant. If nothing else, it will give you a perspective on recent history, stir your thinking, and help you see the world through other people's eyes. It might also change how you see yourself.

337. In case it needs to be said, use *Oriental* to describe rugs, and *Asian* to describe people.

338.

See every person as having something to teach you.

339. Think about the impact of your words, not just your intent. And don't ever forget the power of listening, especially to another person's experience or viewpoint.

340. Don't be so afraid of innocent mistakes that you forget how to laugh.

When my cousin Janis and I were in college, Janis went to work as a housecleaner for a grad student from Saudi Arabia. The very first day, as she went about her work, he walked up to her and asked, "Why are you dusting with my turban?"

341. Don't make someone feel "other" or less than because they don't celebrate your holidays. When the time is right, show a polite interest in *their* holidays.

342. If you don't already have a passport, get one now, so you'll have it when you need it.

343. Learn at least the basics of another language and culture.

Funny side-note: I once overheard the following exchange between two male friends of mine, the first in his twenties and the second in his forties.

"I can say 'I love you' in forty-eight different languages!"

"I have a helluva time saying it in one."

344. Anytime you're visiting another country, research and respect the local customs.

345. Familiarize yourself with Oberg's Stages of Assimilation.

Due to intellectual property laws, I don't think I'm allowed to reprint them here. But if you do a Google search, they should pop right up. Knowing these stages will help you make sense of your transition to another culture, or any other transition. I know they helped me with my adjustment to California and readjustment to Michigan.

Bottom line: The honeymoon doesn't last—but fortunately, neither does the crisis stage. Best not to take either one too terribly seriously.

Free online bonus: Grab a link to Oberg's Stages of Assimilation at ultimatereminders.com/free-college-downloads.

346. When in Rome, don't look for an Olive Garden.

347. Commit yourself to learning more about other worlds (and yourself) for the rest of your life.

Life Stuff

In times of stress, it's all too easy to put our lives on hold—but I don't recommend it. For example, as I finished this book, I could have stayed in my pajamas, cut off contact with the outside world, and survived on Hostess Cupcakes. I didn't. Though come to think of it, that last part does sound sort of tempting, especially with good, strong coffee.

348. Before you pursue your dreams, count the cost.

For example, if you want a big family and you also want to be a heart surgeon, decide which one matters more. It may be tough to excel at both.

349. If you're single, enjoy being single.

350. If you have to choose between having a class ring and having class, choose the latter.

One way we demonstrate class is by how we treat other people, especially those who can't help us get ahead—or who can't help us at all.

351. Show respect for good work, whether or not it requires formal schooling.

"If a man is called to be a street sweeper, he should sweep streets even as a Michelangelo painted, or Beethoven composed music, or Shakespeare wrote poetry. He should sweep streets so well that all the hosts of heaven and earth will pause to say, 'Here lived a great street sweeper who did his job well.'"

– Dr. Martin Luther King Jr.

352. Do your own work, regardless of how menial, with dignity, integrity, and purpose.

Yes, even if it's bussing tables, packing peaches, and cleaning public toilets—all of which I did in high school/college, though fortunately on different days.

353. Accept that grief is messy and hard.

Don't judge yourself for not moving through it well enough or fast enough. I have never known grief to take less time than anticipated to work through. It might even take a lifetime.

354. Don't let activity become a substitute for action.

As someone once told me, "You can read all the books you want on how to swim—eventually, you've got to get into the water."

355. Learn to appreciate, make, and share good food.

Not necessarily elaborate food—just good. It helps if you've worked in a restaurant, but you can also learn from books, YouTube, your family, and your own experimentation. Have fun with it.

356. Make meals more exciting by including a variety of textures, temperatures, colors, and tastes.

A few examples:

- Baked chicken breast, roasted vegetables, applesauce, and a side salad
- Chicken piccata, steamed broccoli, and a side of pasta with butter, Parmesan, and freshly ground black pepper
- Scrambled eggs, sautéed spinach, fresh fruit, toast, and coffee

Special thanks to my mom for imparting this lesson so I could pass it on to you.

Gina's Chicken Piccata

Prep Time: 20 Minutes

Servings: 2

2 boneless, skinless chicken breasts (about 4 oz. each), flattened or sliced thin

Flour

1 tablespoon olive oil

1 tablespoon butter or margarine

Salt and freshly ground pepper to taste

½ teaspoon dried basil

1 fresh lemon, washed and cut in half

3 tablespoons capers, drained

As with most recipes, this will go a lot faster if you get all the ingredients measured out and ready before moving on to the steps below.

1. Heat oil and butter in a 10-inch skillet over medium heat.

2. Spread a handful or two of flour onto a plate, and dredge chicken pieces in flour, shaking off excess before placing chicken pieces in hot oil.

3. As soon as chicken is in the pan, add salt, pepper, and basil. Increase heat if necessary to brown chicken on both sides.

4. As soon as the chicken is browned, reduce heat to low and squeeze juice from both lemon halves through a strainer, over the chicken.

5. Sprinkle capers over chicken pieces, cover and shut off heat for 5 minutes.

6. Enjoy!

Chicken should be cooked to an internal temperature of 165 degrees. When in doubt, use a meat thermometer.

357. If someone's nice enough to give you a plate of brownies, make sure you wash and dry the plate before returning it.

358. Always look for what you *can* do, not at what you can't.

Maybe you can't play collegiate sports, but you can probably play intramurals. And if you're like me and can't do either one, there's a good chance we could be friends.

359. Don't let *anyone* tell you to write like someone else, think like someone else, or be like someone else.

You're you—irreplaceable you—and you're here to set the world on fire. You don't do that by trying to meet the world's false expectations.

360. Play to your strengths, not your weaknesses. Sometimes the only difference between the two is context.

Once, when I "just missed" getting accepted into a highly prestigious Master of Fine Arts program, the director told me nicely that my professional newsletter-writing came through in my efforts at creative nonfiction.

He was right. Newsletter-writing is, by nature, pithy and unadorned.

Creative nonfiction, on the other hand, is elaborate and full of sensory detail. To this day, I still couldn't describe a grassy knoll if I tried. There are writers who can do that sort of thing with relative ease, and make it meaningful. I'm just not one of them. And at long last, I'm okay with that.

361. Learn from other people's experience.

"As a parent of thirteen-year-old quadruplets (three boys and one girl) and as a bone marrow transplant survivor (thirteen years and counting), I know firsthand how life experiences build one's mind, soul, and character.

These experiences don't just prepare you for how to handle the high moments of life, but also how to survive the difficult moments. As many of us have found out the hard way, one can't appreciate success unless we have lived and survived difficult and trying times.

I certainly wouldn't wish chemotherapy, a bone marrow transplant, and the recovery with its ups and downs on anyone. But having endured, survived, and lived through the good days and the bad days for more than four thousand days since my transplant, I feel that I have grown as a person and have a greater appreciation for many of the things others take for granted.

Like Saul and the life-changing event he experienced on the road to Damascus, we don't know when and how that life-changing experience may enter our life. Saul, the one-time enemy of Jesus, became Paul and the greatest missionary that ever lived on this earth.

Until a life-changing event enters your life, you must prepare for the good and the bad and hopefully build a base or foundation to draw from. In the end, it is that foundation and base that will enable you to see and achieve success in anything you are confronted with."

– William R., CPA

362. When you meet someone who is good, kind, and willing to help you, do everything you reasonably can to make them glad they did.

363. Rule #1 for handling a critic: Consider the source.

364. Be a world citizen.

Each of us is called to different forms of global commitment, but each of us can and should do something. A few possibilities:

- Sponsoring a child overseas
- Visiting someone in a local nursing home
- Contributing time or money to organizations that help people help themselves

365. Fall down ten times, get back up eleven.

366. Don't be anyone's sycophant.

367. Don't answer the phone when you're naked.

368. Take notes on everything life teaches you.

369.

Change course if you have to, but never, ever give up hope.

Final Thoughts

As God is my witness, just as I started writing you this quasi-benediction, "Church" by Lyle Lovett came on my iPhone. *So* great.

In that spirit, allow me to wish for you an amazing life. May you make wise decisions, surround yourself with true friends, learn from your mistakes, triumph over adversity, live to have the last laugh, and otherwise go forth and kick butt.

May you grow to be enlightened, not just educated. May your college years help you build a strong foundation—mentally, physically, emotionally, economically, spiritually, and morally—for the rest of your life and for future generations.

Finally, thank you for the privilege of influencing your life. Because of you, I have more than a career. I have a calling. May these pages inspire you to hold fast to *your* calling, and fulfill it with all your heart.

With all *my* heart,

Gina

P.S. If you like what you've read, please help me spread the word. Also be sure to sign up for my newsletter at UltimateReminders.com. I'm always giving away free stuff, and it's a fun way for us to stay in touch.

Acknowledgments

To my parents, **Jim and Judy DeLapa,** who blazed the trail for all of us by being the first in their families to go to college, against all odds. You rock, and I love you forever.

Special shout-out to my dad for launching a one-man campaign on my behalf, before the first iteration of this book even hit the shelves.[8] I also wish to thank the friends, family, and fambly who put the book into the hands of hundreds of students, nationwide. Finally, to Jared Kuritz, who moved heaven and earth to make it happen.

To **all who shared their insights and reflections,** well, the privilege is mine. On behalf of those whose lives you will touch, *thank you.*

Gratitude-beyond-words also belongs to the faculty, staff, and students in the **University of San Diego graduate counseling program** and to **USD Career Services.** Some of the best advice I ever heard was, "Don't dork out." Yet that's exactly what I want to do, each time I recall how you made it possible for me to teach and counsel college students. *Thank you for changing my life.*

To **Monkey C Media, Jared Kuritz of STRATEGIES, and Mary Altbaum,** who have been here from the start. Heartfelt thanks for all the kindness you have shown and the countless miracles you have worked on my behalf.

To the Author of Life (Acts 3:15) and source of all my joy.
As always, I offer You everything.

8. Download the whole crazy story ("A Father's Generosity—On Steroids") at ultimatereminders.com/free-college-downloads.

Recommended Reads

Bolles, Richard Nelson. *What Color Is Your Parachute?* Berkeley, CA: Ten Speed Press, 2015.

Bruni, Frank. *Where You Go Is Not Who You'll Be: An Antidote to the College Admissions Mania.* New York: Grand Central Publishing, 2015.

De Becker, Gavin. *The Gift of Fear: Survival Signals That Protect Us From Violence.* New York: Dell Publishing, 1998.

Pipher, Mary. *Letters to a Young Therapist.* New York: Basic Books, 2003.

Reynolds, Garr. *Presentation Zen: Simple Ideas on Presentation Design and Delivery.* Berkeley, CA: New Riders, 2008.

Robinson, Adam. *What Smart Students Know: Maximum Grades. Optimum Learning. Minimum Time.* New York: Three Rivers Press, 1993.

Schwartz, Tony, Jean Gomes, and Catherine McCarthy. *The Way We're Working Isn't Working: The Four Forgotten Needs That Energize Great Performance.* New York: Free Press, 2010.

Tulgan, Bruce. *Not Everyone Gets a Trophy: How to Manage Generation Y.* San Francisco, CA: Jossey-Bass, 2009.

Yate, Martin. *Knock'em Dead 2015: The Ultimate Job Search Guide.* Avon, MA: Adams Media, 2015.

Also by Gina DeLapa

Part pep talk, part reflection, part friendly kick in the rear, *Ultimate Reminders for Everyday Life* gives you 437 ways to make your life more meaningful and fun—from doing the right thing (#256) to setting boundaries (#332) to relating to people half your age (#369).

No matter what your season of life—whether newly graduated, climbing the corporate ladder, or living out your legacy years—*Ultimate Reminders for Everyday Life* is sure to spark laughter, conversation, contemplation, and bold new action. Order your copies today!